A TEST OF YOUR ANIMAL INSTINCTS

1. **Approximately how much food does a full-grown elephant eat per day?**
2. **How does an armadillo get across rivers?**
3. **What bird flies in first-class comfort?**
4. **How does the male African hornbill keep the female in line after mating?**
5. **What determines the gender of alligators?**
6. **How do hornets amuse themselves?**

Answers

1. **400 pounds worth.** In the Bronx Zoo, elephants are fed 300 pounds of hay, 16 quarts of grain, and 16 quarts of carrots, apples, and stale Italian bread.
2. He gulps down air until his stomach is like a balloon, and then he floats across.
3. The albatross, a bird that can doze while he flies.
4. He plasters her up in the hollow of a tree and doesn't release her until the eggs are hatched.
5. **The temperature.** If the eggs are incubated below 86 degrees Fahrenheit, then females are born; above 93, and the offspring are male.
6. They drink themselves silly, swilling the juices of fermented fruit until they fall into a stupor.

ELEPHANTS CAN'T JUMP

& OTHER FREAKY FACTS ABOUT ANIMALS

Barbara Seuling

IVY BOOKS • NEW YORK

to Gwenn, my zoo pal, niece,
conspirator, French tutor, and good friend,
with love

Contents

ELEPHANTS CAN'T JUMP

& OTHER FREAKY FACTS ABOUT ANIMALS

1

TOOTH AND NAIL

Physical Characteristics

○ Elephants can't jump. Although they have the same bones in their feet as other animals, theirs are more closely packed, giving them none of the flexibility or spring mechanism that enables others to jump.

○ The shark's skin is covered with denticles, tiny little teeth, which can scrape the skin off a human brushing against them. Some people believe that ancient Roman soldiers wore helmets made of sharkskin.

○ The sperm whale has the largest brain of any mammal. The largest sperm whale brain on record weighs a little more than 17 pounds.

○ The giraffe has the same number of neck bones as a mouse—seven.

○ Shells of giant clams have been used as holy water fonts in European churches. Giant land tortoise shells have been used as bathtubs.

○ Woodpeckers don't get headaches when they hammer continually on hard wood because their skull bones contain many air spaces which act as shock absorbers.

○ The shark doesn't have a bone in its body: Its skeleton is made completely of cartilage. The sea horse has a skeleton, but it's on the outside.

○ The octopus once had a shell, like the snail, the clam, and the oyster. Its tentacles grew as its shell got smaller, and eventually the shell disappeared.

○ For years, it was believed that giraffes made no sound at all. A study was made, and it turns out that the giraffe can, indeed, make sounds as other animals do, but it just doesn't care to. Giraffes prefer body language when talking to other giraffes.

○ The skin of the moloch, an Australian lizard, is like a blotter. If the animal stands in water so that only its feet are submerged, soon its skin is wet all over.

○ The barn owl's face, shaped like a dish, collects sounds like a radar screen.

○ The Komodo dragon, the largest lizard on earth, is 10 feet long and weighs as much as 250 pounds.

○ The lips of a hippopotamus are nearly 2 feet wide.

○   Birds can sing more than one song apiece. The robin and the meadowlark, for example, have about fifty different songs. Some bird couples sing duets, each bird singing different notes. It is almost impossible to tell where one bird leaves off and another begins.

○   The wings of bats are actually membranes of skin connecting long, slender fingers.

○ The kiwi of Australia has only tiny wing sprouts and cannot fly like other birds, but it also has something no other bird has: nostrils at the tip of its beak to help it sniff worms underground.

○ The tuatara lizard of New Zealand has three eyes—two in the usual place, and one on the top of its head. Other vertebrates, long extinct, had a functional third eye, but this is the only living creature in which it now exists.

○ The dugong, a large, gentle marine mammal, sheds tears when it is in trouble or pain. At one time, the animal was captured and tortured to collect its tears, which were then sold as love charms.

○ A species of salamander called the Proteus, or cave newt, is born with tiny eyes which eventually disappear. Its whole life is spent in dark underground caves.

○ The Falabella horse of Argentina, when full grown, is about as big as a German shepherd.

○ Elephant tusks are actually teeth and sometimes grow 11 feet long. The inside molars are as big as bricks. When an elephant has a toothache, he has a big problem. If the root of a tusk is infected, the pain can be so great that the elephant will extract the tooth—or tusk—himself, by wedging it in the crotch of a tree and pulling.

○ Snow fleas, which live 22,000 feet above sea level in the Himalayas, freeze solid each night, when the temperature drops drastically, and thaw out the next day.

○ The koala has an appendix that is 6 to 8 feet long.

○ Moose are so nearsighted that some have mistaken automobiles for their mates.

○ A shark may have twenty-four thousand teeth —all razor sharp—in its lifetime.

○ A beaver must chew wood every day, or its teeth would grow so long it would not be able to eat, and it would starve to death. One beaver chews down hundreds of trees in a year.

○ The yak's milk is pink.

○ Dogs sweat through their foot pads. Cows sweat through their noses. Hippopotamuses sweat all over—in red when they are excited. The color is from an oily secretion that keeps a hippo's hide from drying and cracking.

○ Some animals have rarely been seen alive— the giant squid, for example. Dead specimens show that it can reach a length of 55 feet and has eyes 9 inches across. Longman's beaked whale has never been seen alive. It is known only from two skulls that washed ashore, one in Australia in 1926 and one in East Africa in 1955.

○ Cows give more milk when they listen to music. Some cows show a distinct preference for Mozart.

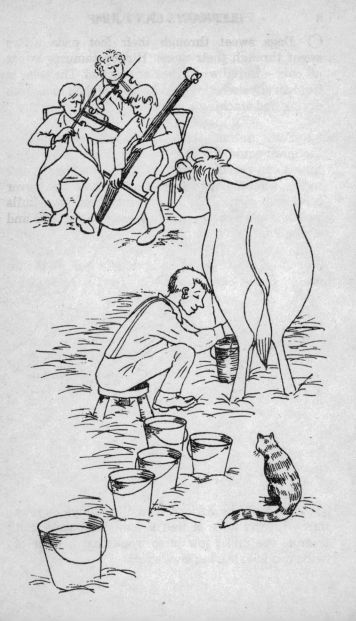

○ Although the African crocodile clamps its jaws shut with the force of half a ton, the muscle that controls the upper jaw is so weak that a piece of twine can hold the big jaws shut.

○ The jellyfish is 95 percent water.

○ If the lowly sponge is squeezed through very fine mesh and divided into thousands of separate bits, the cells will rejoin to form the same sponge, identical to the original in every way.

2

HOME SWEET HOME

Dwellings

○ Inside the Carlsbad Caverns in New Mexico, where millions of bats make their home, each bat hangs in one square inch of space.

○ Tailor ants, found in Australia, Africa, and India, use their own offspring to sew together leaves for their nests. For thread, they use the silken threads secreted by their larvae. For needles, they use the larvae themselves, pushing them in and out of the holes in the leaves.

○ Although the mounds of magnetic termites in Australia may be 20 feet high and solid enough for elephants to use as scratching posts, they are only a few inches across. The skinny sides are exposed to the direct rays of the sun during the hottest part of the day, keeping the mound from overheating. In the morning and late afternoon, the cooler times of the day, the wider sides are exposed. It is a perfect example of a solar home, obtaining the maximum benefit from the sun's rays to keep temperatures inside the mound at a comfortable level.

◯ Some hermit crabs have made their homes in soup cans. Having no shells of their own to protect their soft and vulnerable bodies from enemies, they usually "borrow" the cast-off shells of other creatures. When they are young, this is easy, but as they grow, they must move to larger and larger homes, and large shells are hard to find. Some crabs will use anything that can be made into a dwelling, including coconut shells, parts of lamps, plaster models—and soup cans.

◯ There is a luminous glowworm found in only one spot on earth—the subterranean depths of New Zealand's Waitomo Caverns. Resembling twinkling stars in the darkness of the caves, the tiny creatures use their lights to lure prey to them.

○ Shortly after they are born, barnacles glue themselves to a surface and stay in that one place for life. The substance they use to bond themselves to their permanent address is about twice the strength of epoxy and stronger than any glue manufactured by man.

○ The chipmunk builds his home complete with indoor plumbing. The underground dwelling has a separate chamber off the bedroom that serves as a bathroom and drains into the ground away from the living quarters.

○ Some alligators live in nests that are a thousand years old.

○ Weaverbirds build huge condominiums—communal dwellings like apartment houses—that contain nearly a hundred separate nests.

○ Pupfish have the most restricted home on earth. They live only in one place—the pools on a rock shelf in the Amargosa Desert in Ash Meadows, Nevada.

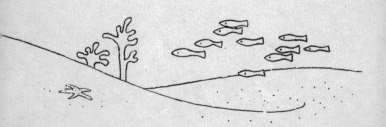

○ The fox squirrel builds its home on the same principle as that for thermal underwear: It is insulated in a manner that makes use of dead-air spaces.

○ Sponges serve as apartment houses for very small sea animals. The sponge's passageways provide many compartments in which the tiny creatures can make their homes.

○ The peregrine falcon, which usually nests in high cliffs and canyons across the United States, has been known to nest on the windowsills of skyscrapers in New York City. The bird finds the windowsills a good substitute when it is away from home.

○ During the day, the oilbird of South America lives deep inside mountain caves where it is totally dark. At dusk, the oilbird flies out only to search for food, then returns to the cave.

○ Bee hives are air-conditioned. In hot weather bees place drops of water or diluted honey around the hive and fan their wings, keeping the hive cool.

○ Mole rats of East Africa live in underground colonies in much the same way that some insects do, conducting their lives in subterranean chambers within a large society headed by a queen.

○ Kirtland's warbler, an endangered bird, depends on forest fires for its survival. Only the intense heat of such a fire can burst open the tight cones of the jack pine tree, dispersing its seeds. These seeds eventually grow into a new forest of young pines, where the bird thrives. When the trees grow too tall, the birds leave.

○ There can be eighty thousand bees living in one hive.

○ The African lovebird, a small parrot, cuts leaves into long strips with its beak, then tucks these strips into its feathers to fly them to its home-building site, where they are used for nesting material.

○   Ross's seal does not live on land or in the water; it lives exclusively on the floating ice of the Ross Sea in the Antarctic.

○   The bald eagle builds and adds on to a nest until it is about 12 feet deep and 8½ feet wide—about the same size as the average child's room.

○   Army ants build houses out of their own suspended bodies, each one clinging to another. Within this living structure, a queen is sheltered, and young are born and raised.

○   The prairie dog's burrow is a 12-foot hole, straight down, into which the animal dives head first.

○ Once beavers decide on a site for their home, they cannot be persuaded to change their minds— not with dynamite, traps, or even floods. The only thing that will make beavers leave their home is lack of food.

3

TASTY TIDBITS

Eating Habits

○   The panda's diet is almost exclusively bamboo, and it can consume about 90 pounds of it a day, which is one reason why pandas are hard to keep in captivity.

○   A full-grown elephant eats about 400 pounds of food a day. In the jungle, this consists of leaves, fruits, grasses, twigs, and bark. At the Bronx Zoo in New York, the elephants are fed 300 pounds of hay, 16 quarts of grain, and 16 quarts of carrots, apples, and stale Italian bread.

○   Some ants become living storage tanks to hold food for the whole colony's use in emergencies. They eat until they grow into such huge balls that they can hardly move. During hard times, they regurgitate the stored food.

○ Termites eat wood. However, without the help of certain microorganisms that live inside them, they would not be able to digest it. They would eat and eat and eat—and still starve to death.

○ Two-headed snakes are occasionally born. The two heads fight over food, even though it will go into the one stomach that they share. When they are really angry, they might try to swallow each other. Normal snakes will sometimes swallow snakes longer than themselves.

○ The pouch under a pelican's bill can hold up to 25 pounds of fish, or 3 gallons of water.

○ The anglerfish has a kind of fishing rod growing out of its head, with a lure at the end to attract its victims.

○ Leopards take their prey up into a tree to eat it. Sometimes, the meal can be a baby giraffe or antelope that is bigger than the leopard itself.

○ Ants have devised many clever ways to secure a food supply. Some keep gardens where they collect bits of leaves to compost for the raising of mushrooms. Some raise herds of aphids, which they milk for their nutritious secretions. Others, more aggressive, make war and raid and loot the seed and grain warehouses of other ant colonies.

○ Wolves and wild dogs are able to swallow food, which fills their bellies but remains undigested, while they are out hunting. When they arrive home, they then disgorge the undigested food to feed their young and those who stayed at home to guard the den.

○ Hedgehogs have been known to steal milk directly from the cow.

○ There are crabs that climb trees to snip off coconuts.

○ To crack open an egg, the Egyptian vulture throws stones at it.

○ Sled dogs can get drunk from eating fresh shark meat, which is toxic.

○ The tiny shrew has such a delicate nervous system and metabolism that, unless it eats every hour or two, it will starve to death.

○ Crows have been seen stealing bait and fish from fishing lines left in holes in the ice in Norway and Sweden. They draw in the lines with their beaks and hold them down with their feet to keep them from slipping back into the water.

○ A heron, wading in the water, will hold a small feather in its beak and watch quietly for a fish to go by. When it spots one, it drops the feather. As the fish goes toward the lure, the heron snatches it.

○ Coyotes in Los Angeles have been known to sneak into the backyards of wealthy homes at night and sip water from the swimming pools.

○ Alligators weed their waterholes constantly, to keep them free of tangled seaweed and water lily stems, so that turtles—the alligators' favorite food—will have a clear place to swim.

○ Unfortunately, the leatherback turtle loves to eat jellyfish. Plastic bags, which look like jellyfish floating on the surface of the water, get swallowed by the huge turtles, causing serious internal distress.

○ Victims of the giant water bug present an eerie spectacle. The beetle paralyzes its victim—a frog, perhaps—then sucks the juices out of its body, so that all that is left looks every bit like the original frog, but is actually only an empty shell which collapses at the slightest touch.

○ Light fish, which live along the Indonesian coral reefs, have built-in searchlights under their eyes, which help them search for food by beaming light through the water. The light is given off by luminescent bacteria that collect in pouches under the fish's eyes.

4

A LITTLE TRAVELING MUSIC, PLEASE

Getting Around

○ Spiny lobsters march in caravan fashion when they migrate, each lobster latching on to the one in front of it. They march so doggedly that when a group of them was removed from the sea and placed in a vinyl pool for an experiment, they kept going around and around, single file, for two weeks.

○ Some South African shrews are so small that they travel through tunnels dug by earthworms.

○ Penguins can't fly, but when they are underwater, they swim as though they were in flight, their flippers and feet propelling them swiftly through the water. Some penguins dive deeper than can people equipped with scuba gear.

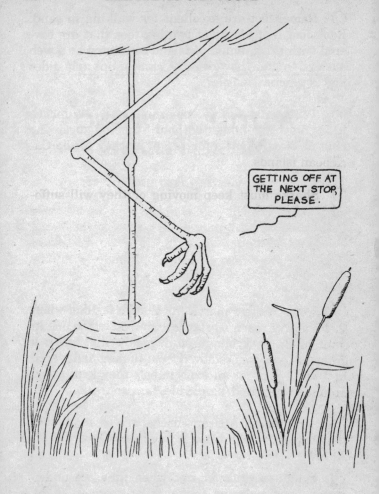

○ Tiny snails embed themselves in the mud on the feet of wading birds. When the birds move, the snails get a free ride.

○ Camel feet are excellent for walking in sand. Each foot is made up of two big toes that are covered with thick, tough pads and connected by a web of skin. In mud, however, the camel slips and slides and is practically helpless.

○ The hummingbird, sometimes only 2½ inches long, flies 500 miles, without stopping, over the Gulf of Mexico on its migration journey to the Caribbean islands.

○ Sharks must keep moving or they will suffocate. Other fish have air bladders that enable them to breathe even when they are still. Sharks do not have this device, so when they stop moving, water can't flow over their gills to supply them with oxygen, which they need to live.

○ Most rabbits are helpless in water, but one species, the marsh rabbit of the southeastern United States, swims and dives. When it wants to rest, it builds a raft of reeds, climbs aboard, and sails along.

○ Cats have whiskers on the back of their front legs, as well as around their mouths. Their leg whiskers pick up air vibrations and help them get around in the dark.

○ Before monarch butterflies make a long journey, they sunbathe to gather enough heat to warm up their thoracic muscles, which control their wings.

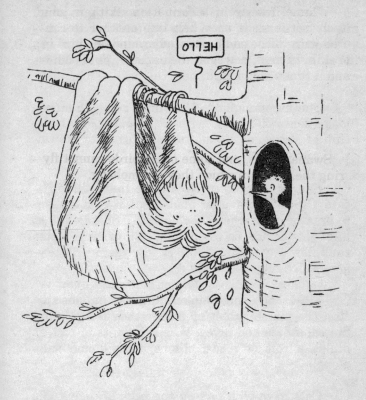

○ Creeping slowly from one branch to another, the sloth rarely comes down out of the trees even for a drink. If it does land on the ground, it has to walk on the sides of its feet, because its toes are permanently curved under into a hooked position. These hooks enable the animal to hang upside down securely, from which position it eats, sleeps, mates, and even gives birth.

○ When birds fly in V formation on their long migration journeys, they help one another to conserve energy. The eddies created around one bird in flight help the bird just behind it. The eddies around that bird, in turn, help the next in line, and so forth. The only one who gets no help is the leader, at the head of the V, so he is replaced often by another bird.

○ Swans, ducks, and some other birds cannot fly during the period in which they are molting.

○ African jacanas, birds also known as lily-trotters, walk across lily pads on their long toes without sinking.

○ The only way a bat can get started in flight is to drop from its sleeping perch into the air. Once it is flying, it cannot stop until it is ready to latch on to another perch.

○ The ostrich can run as fast as a racehorse.

○ Wolves can travel a distance of 30 to 40 miles in a single night.

○ The huge albatross, the world's largest flying creature, with a wingspan of 12 feet, is dependent on the wind for flight. Without a breeze, it cannot move and is trapped on the ocean until a wind strong enough to enable it to lift off comes along.

◯ Mudskippers of Australia, Africa, and Asia are fish that live in rivers, but when the rivers dry up, the fish "row" across land until they come to more water. Some even climb trees in their travels.

◯ To swim across a river, an armadillo gulps air until its stomach is full, then slides into the water and floats across like a balloon.

5

NOW I LAY ME
DOWN TO SLEEP

Sleeping Habits

○ The huge albatross can sleep while it flies. Helped by the updraft of airwaves, the bird can doze at a speed of 25 miles an hour.

○ The lungfish lives through the dry season in Africa by burrowing down into the mud, curling up in a ball, and sealing itself in with a layer of its own slime. Inside this cozy shelter, it goes to sleep. As the water dries up, the mud hardens around it in a clay coating. When the rainy season comes, the water softens the clay and the fish emerges, alive and well. European explorers used to ship these hard balls of clay home, where they would be dropped in water and, as the clay dissolved, release a live fish.

◯ The tuatara lizard of New Zealand sleeps about 90 percent of the time. It is so lethargic that it sometimes falls asleep in the middle of dinner.

◯ Although all animals rest sometimes, it is believed that some do not really sleep. Goats, for example, rest about eight hours a day, but they never close their eyes and are constantly alert.

◯ Horses, giraffes, and some other four-legged animals sleep standing up, although the giraffe will sometimes lean against a tree. Elephants usually sleep standing up, otherwise they might crush themselves. If they do lie down, they have to rock themselves from side to side to get their big bodies upright again.

◯ When a gorilla family goes to bed, they make a nest of branches and leaves in the crotch of a tree. If the male is really heavy, he may be too big for the tree, and he may sleep at the base of it. This led observers to believe that the male gorilla was guarding his family. The family rarely stays in the same place two nights in a row.

◯ When sea otters go to sleep at night, they wrap themselves in long strands of kelp, to keep from being separated from their companions. During the night, they may drift miles out to sea, tied together in the seaweed.

◯ Many animals hibernate, or sleep through the winter, but none sleep as soundly as the bat. Some have been found coated with ice, yet awaken as good as new when the weather gets warm.

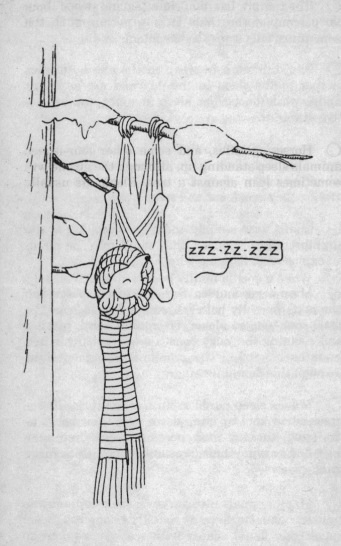

◯ Birds don't fall off their perches when they sleep because their toes lock in place around the twig or branch on which they sit.

◯ One difference between moths and butterflies is that moths sleep in the day and are active at night, while butterflies sleep at night and are active during the day.

◯ Parrot fish, which live in undersea coral caves, pull a blanket of mucus, or slime, over themselves when they go to sleep. In the morning, when they awake, they break out and swim away.

◯ Quails form a circle and go to sleep, but at the slightest hint of danger, they burst into the air in an explosion of flapping wings.

◯ After a good meal, the crocodile naps on the banks of the river with its jaws agape. In hops the little spur-winged plover, or crocodile bird, picking and cleaning the huge beast's teeth, getting a free meal as it works. The crocodile can sleep right through this dental flossing.

◯ Wolves sleep outdoors in temperatures 40 degrees below zero by lying down with their backs to the wind, tucking their noses between their rear legs, and burying their faces under their thick furry tails.

6

YOU WERE MEANT FOR ME

Perpetuating the Race

○ After mating, the male African hornbill plasters up his mate in the hollow of a tree or cave. Only a small opening remains, through which he passes food to her. Inside, the brooding female lays her eggs, not breaking out until the eggs are hatched.

○ Male spiders are often eaten by the female immediately after mating, so they have developed devious means to ensure their survival. The male of one species presents the female with a carefully wrapped "wedding" present, usually a fly, and hopes that he will have time to mate with her and escape with his life before she finishes unwrapping his gift.

○ Certain fish off the California coast come onto the beaches once each year during high tide, riding the waves in to shore by the thousands, to lay their eggs in the sand. These fish, called grunions, spawn in holes drilled by the females, and ride back out to sea on the next huge wave, leaving the eggs to develop in the sand and be carried back out to sea when they are about to hatch.

◯ Male bowerbirds of Australia and New Guinea construct elaborate courting palaces to which they lure females in order to mate. The bowers are carefully constructed, sometimes big enough for a human to enter, and are decorated with brightly colored or glittering objects—bits of colored glass, beetle wings, bleached bones, feathers, berries, and plastic toys. Fresh flowers are also used, and are replaced when they begin to wilt. Some birds even paint their walls with paintbrushes made from twigs stripped of bark, dipped in a mixture of saliva and charcoal or berry juice.

◯ The swordtail fish of Mexico changes sex in the middle of its life. While it is female, it has babies. When it becomes a male, it fertilizes eggs.

◯ Most male seals and sea lions are bachelors. In a herd, only about 4 percent of the males mate with the females and produce offspring, fighting off all those smaller and weaker males who compete with them.

◯ Some animals have been crossed with each other successfully. A lion and a tiger, for example, produced a liger; a leopard and a jaguar have produced a jagulep; and a zebra and a donkey—a zeedonk. Usually the offspring of such crosses are

sterile, otherwise zoos would be filled with such creatures as ligerjaguleps.

○ Female sea horses lay their eggs directly into the male's pouch, and he carries them around until they hatch.

○ The mayfly has only two hours to spend on this earth, and uses them for just one purpose—mating. It does not even have a working mouth, because it doesn't need one: It has no time to eat.

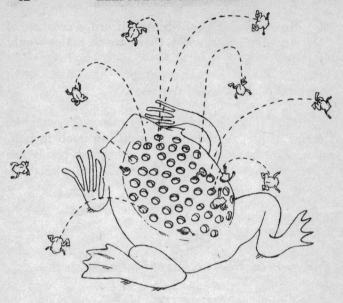

○ The Surinam toad spreads fertilized eggs over the female's back. The eggs settle into little pockets in her skin where they develop and hatch, at which point tiny little toads seem to burst out of their mother's back.

○ Right after he hatches, the male anglerfish grabs onto his sister with his teeth and hangs on for dear life, until the skin of the female actually grows around him, and he becomes a part of her. As the female grows, the male remains a small appendage growing out of her skin, becoming useful only when he is needed to fertilize her eggs.

○ In some species of whiptail lizard, a creature of the American Southwest, there are no males—only females. They give birth to females—by means of a process called parthenogenesis—and these give birth to more females, and so on.

○ The single-celled amoeba, among the simplest forms of life, reproduces by splitting itself in half. For some reason, the two halves that result are younger than the original "parent"; these must develop and mature before they are able to divide again.

○ Computers are being used to bring animals together for "dates." This system may be the only means of survival for some endangered species.

7

IN THE NURSERY

Baby Care

○ A crocodile's first bath takes place in its mother's jaws. The mother crocodile watches her nest deep in the sand, for signs that her eggs are ready to hatch. When the babies appear, she takes them in her teeth, marches down to the water, and swishes them around in her mouth to wash off all the sand.

○ When they are a little older, baby crocodiles thrash around in the water doing the dog paddle to stay afloat. Only after they swallow some stones, which are used for digestion, do they gain the proper balance to swim horizontally.

○ The embryos of sand tiger sharks fight one another in the womb until only one is left at the time of birth.

○ Armadillo mothers almost always have four babies at a time, all the same sex, and identical in every way, down to the exact number of hairs on their undersides.

○   Some baby birds have a strong instinct to follow the first moving thing they see after they are born, as though it were their mother. Ducks in Bali have followed a flag stuck on a pole and have stayed within sight of it while they grazed in the rice fields.

○   When an alligator's eggs are incubated below 86 degrees Fahrenheit, all females are born. If the temperature is above 93 degrees, the offspring are male. This oddity may be a clue to why dinosaurs became extinct. A severe climate change could have resulted in several generations of one type of offspring, permitting no procreation and eventually killing off the species.

○   The cuckoo doesn't build its own nest. Instead, it leaves its eggs in another bird's nest, sometimes tossing out eggs that are already there. The foster mother cares for the orphans, although they may be twice her size. If the cuckoo parent does not get rid of the competition, the hatchlings do the job, nudging their stepbrothers and stepsisters to the edge of the nest and pushing them out.

○   Megapodes, big thick-legged birds of Australia and the South Pacific, lay their eggs on a heap of rotting vegetation. The heat from the mass incubates and hatches the eggs. With their responsibilities behind them, the parent birds take off, never returning. Fortunately, the young are born ready to take care of themselves. A minute after hatching, a young bird can fly.

○ The female porcupine is not injured by its baby's quills when giving birth because, for the first few moments of life, the newborn porcupine's quills are soft.

○ A baby blue whale starts out at about 4,000 pounds and gains an additional 200 pounds a day until it reaches its full growth, which is about 150 tons, or 300,000 pounds.

○ Baby giraffes drop several feet to the ground when they are born.

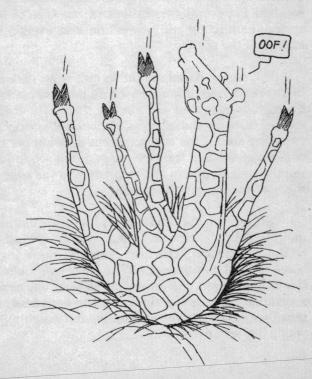

○ One species of bee manufactures tiny bags out of polyester materials with "zip" seals at the top, in which it keeps its larvae safe and dry.

○ Koala babies ride around in backseats, because their mothers' pouches are on backward. The tiny embryo crawls from the mother's womb when it is only thirty-two or thirty-three days old, heading up toward the rear pouch, where it fastens on a teat.

○ Some female animals, including bears, weasels, and seals, carry a spare embryo; if something happens to one baby, the spare develops to take its place.

○ Although the codfish lays about 4 million eggs a year, only one will probably survive to become an adult fish. The ling fish lays about 30 million eggs, and only two may survive.

○ A kangaroo mother almost always has babies of different ages and has two different supplies of milk. One nipple supplies one formula of milk for the brand-new baby, while another supplies a diluted solution for the older youngster.

○ When baby ostriches are frightened, they squat and flatten themselves out as much as possible, so that they barely cast a shadow.

○ Although they spend most of their lives in the water, sea lions do not swim naturally. Mothers have to teach their babies the fine points of swimming.

○ A baby whale nudges its mother when it is hungry and places its mouth near the slit where the teat is. The teat comes out, and a large squirt of milk is ejected into the calf's mouth.

○ All baby birds are born with a single tooth which helps them peck their way out of their shells. After the big breakout, the egg tooth disappears.

○ Moose mothers sometimes carry their 70-pound babies on their backs to cross wide expanses of water. Elephant mothers have used their tusks as forklifts to carry their babies across rivers.

○ The platypus is, scientifically speaking, a mammal, yet its mammary glands are undeveloped, and it has no nipples. A baby has to nudge its mother into secreting a milky substance, which it then licks off the mother's stomach.

○ The American opossum gives birth to about twenty babies at a time, each the size of a honeybee. Only thirteen can survive, however, because that is the number of nipples on the mother. So there is a kind of race at birth to reach the nipples, and the first thirteen are the winners.

○ When the mother lion goes off to hunt, a baby-sitter—another female—may stay with the cubs. For her pay, she gets a free meal from the mother's catch.

○ A male mouthbreeder fish acts as a sort of garage for as many as four hundred of his offspring at a time, protecting them from harm. If one tiny stranger gets in with the brood, the father spits it out without losing any of his own.

○ The bitterling fish and the mussel, a mollusk, have one of the most peculiar relationships going. The fish lays her eggs inside the mussel's shell, where they hatch. The fry leave their foster home as soon as they can manage on their own. Clamped on to the baby fish, for a ride out to sea, are the offspring of the mussel.

○ The male and female Emperor penguins take turns caring for their egg, which is laid on solid ice. Then the female goes off, while the male rests the egg on top of his feet and keeps it warm with a fold of his belly skin. After two months, the female comes to take her turn, and the male, thin and hungry because he hasn't eaten a thing in all that time, leaves to eat.

8

CAMOUFLAGE AND OTHER NEAT TRICKS

Survival Tactics

○ The horned toad, a lizard of the Southwest and Mexico, shoots a stream of blood from its eyes when it is upset.

○ When threatened, the bombadier beetle blasts its victim with a small explosion of stinging chemicals.

○ A porcupine, with twenty-five thousand sharp quills, each one equipped with one thousand tiny barbs, has few enemies. The fisher, a large weasel, has learned to flip over the porcupine before the porcupine has a chance to shoot its quills.

○ The electric eel, found in rivers of South America, can send off an electric charge of 600 volts, enough to electrocute a man. Some eels are totally blind from eye damage caused by the electrical charges given off by their fellow eels.

○ The spray of skunks that is so repulsive to humans is used among skunks as a perfume to attract mates.

○ Spiders weave signs of warning into their webs to keep birds and large insects from flying into and damaging their webs.

◯ Many lizards, when grabbed by the tail, let their tails snap off and make a fast getaway. A new tail later grows in, but without a bone structure to support it. Until the tail is back to its original size, the lizard suffers a kind of social disgrace and loses its former status in the lizard community.

◯ The assassin bug is a master of disguise. It hides behind the carcasses of its dead enemies, termites, to get nearer to the live termites. When one comes to help cart away the dead body, the assassin bug jumps out and attacks it.

◯ The sound of wolves howling is often the howl of a single wolf. The sound is composed of different harmonics—to give the impression that there are more animals than there actually are.

◯ At the approach of danger, termite guards warn their colleagues by shaking their abdomens against the tunnel walls. The vibrations are picked up and sent further along, and so on, until all members of the colony have received the alert.

◯ The queen bee is the only one in the hive with a reusable stinger. Female worker bees lose their stingers in the flesh of their victims, after which they die. Male bees have no stingers at all. The queen, who uses her stinger mainly to kill off rival queens, can retract her stinger without harm.

◯ Parent birds remove all traces of eggshell from their nests after their young are hatched, since the light color of the shell lining can attract predators.

○ The snowshoe rabbit turns from brown to snowy white in the wintertime, making it practically invisible in the snow.

○ The spider crab is a neat dresser. He cuts off pieces of live sponges and wears them on his back. The sponge pieces grow around him to fit. Since sponges taste awful, most animals leave them alone, so the spider crab, in his dandy new suit of clothes, is protected.

○ According to some experts, dolphins send bubbles to the surface to relay messages—perhaps warnings—to other dolphins. They also emit clicks, but no one has figured out exactly what they mean.

○ The Australian sea dragon, a type of sea horse, has leafy-looking extensions growing out of its body that look just like the vines and leaves of real seaweed. Its only defense is to hide itself from enemies with these parts of its own body.

9

HERE I COME,
READY OR NOT

Antics and Amusements

○ Deer play a game of tag in which the one who is "it" tags the other with its hooves.

○ Otters play shoot-the-chutes, a water-slide game. In winter, they take a few quick short steps, then push off for a long slide across the ice.

○ In the 1950s, a playful dolphin moved in close to the bathers at a New Zealand resort and played actively with the youngsters, even allowing a thirteen-year-old girl to climb on its back and go for rides, holding on to its dorsal fin. Historians report that the same thing happened in the ancient Carthaginian seaside resort of Hippo, on the coast of what is now Tunisia, but the dolphin was such a crowd gatherer that it was shooed away to regain privacy for the bathers.

○   Badgers play leapfrog and turn somersaults on the grass.

○   Spotted skunks do handstands, but that's usually a signal that they are about to spray.

○   Fish have been known to play jokes. For example, some have squirted water at attendants in aquariums.

○ Cubs of the North American gray wolf are encouraged to play when they are young, and adult wolves even dig out playgrounds near the den for the pups, enlarging them as the pups grow. The art of playing doesn't die down when they grow older. Adult wolves are known to play tag, run and chase each other, romp with cubs, scare each other by jumping out of hiding places, and play with sticks and bones.

○ When playing, bears like to tumble down hills head over heels.

○ The lyrebird of Australia mimics just about anything it hears. It can copy the sound of a factory whistle, a timber mill saw, the neighing of a horse, and an automobile horn.

○ Hornets love to get drunk. If they can find fermenting fruit, they drink the intoxicating juices until they fall into a stupor, then wake up and start partying again.

○ Crows have a sense of humor and seem to have a great old time playing pranks. One of their favorite games is sneaking up on a sleeping rabbit or cow and making a racket to wake them.

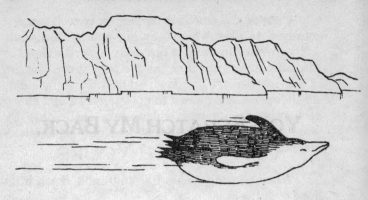

○ Penguins toboggan across the ice on their stomachs.

○ Sea otter mothers float on their backs in the water as they play with their babies, lifting them into the air, fondling and kissing them.

○ Male porcupines will sometimes wrestle for fun, but in order for one to grab the other, they have to be very careful to always face each other. The only place they don't have sharp quills is on their soft bellies.

○ Adult squirrels are very playful, turning somersaults, zipping around in games of chase, rolling in leaves, climbing to the ends of thin, bouncy branches, and swaying playfully in the breeze. They have even been known to use pinecones and paper balls in their games.

10

YOU SCRATCH MY BACK, I'LL SCRATCH YOURS

Peculiar Relationships

◯ Snakes have helped scientists in the study of human diseases and cures. Cobra venom has been found useful in medicine for the relief of severe abdominal pain caused by cancer. The venom of Russell's vipers has been used in the control of hemophilia. Rattlesnake venom is being studied for use in controlling epilepsy.

◯ Seals have been trained by the Navy to work with submarine rockets and mines for undersea war operations.

◯ Poodles were first clipped to make it easier for them to swim. They were brought along by hunters to retrieve birds that were shot down.

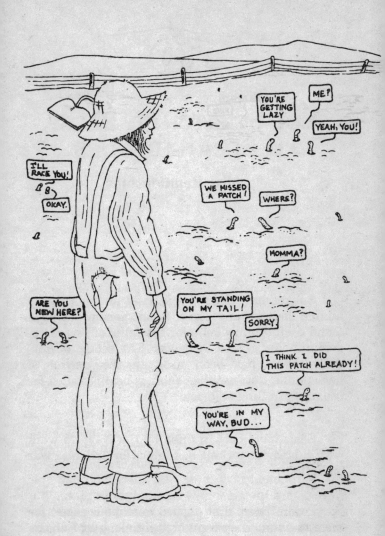

○ Earthworms are a farmer's delight. In one year, the earthworms in an acre of soil can turn over about 18 tons of dirt.

○ A major missile corporation switched from messengers on motorcycles to carrier pigeons to deliver material to its research facility 25 miles away. The pigeons took half the time for a trip and cost a great deal less. Birdfeed for a whole year cost the same as a single day's motorcycle bill.

○ The Aztec Indians of Mexico used little dogs, a tiny Mexican hairless breed, as hot water bottles to warm their feet.

○ Leeches, blood-sucking insects found in the rivers of Africa, were used by European physicians in the Middle Ages to cure all kinds of ailments. For a fever, a band of leeches was placed around the head, where they fastened themselves in place. For indigestion, twenty or thirty were placed on the stomach. In more modern applications, leeches have been used by boxers to drain black eyes, and on patients after plastic surgery.

○ International treaties have been made over the use of guano—bird droppings—which is the richest fertilizer on earth. The largest deposit is off the coast of Peru.

○ Robot designers are studying the spider to design the perfect robotic device. Eight spiderlike legs could alight and walk on almost any uneven surface, an important feature in exploring other planets.

○ A rare kind of silk comes from the *pinnamarina*, or giant silk-bearded clam, found in the Mediterranean Sea. Its milky secretions, in long strands, were once spun into fine cloth and traded in Spain, Italy, and North Africa.

○ New York City has a horse's rights bill. It prohibits working horses in temperatures of 90 degrees or more, and demands that they have a "coffee break"—fifteen minutes' rest for every two hours of work.

○ During the invasion of Normandy in France in 1944, army jeep drivers were helped out in blackouts by glowworms living along the sides of the roads. The tiny lights of these creatures, flashing to attract mates, kept the drivers on the roads.

○ A hand puppet resembling a California condor mother was used to hand-feed a condor chick at the San Diego Zoo. The zoo, dedicated to helping the endangered birds, has a large breeding facility known as the Condorminium.

◯ In a pinch, crickets can substitute for thermometers. Add forty to the number of chirps a cricket makes in fourteen seconds, and the result is the temperature, Fahrenheit, within about 2 degrees.

◯ The chickens we eat today in the United States are descendants of chickens brought here by Christopher Columbus.

11

ONCE UPON A TIME

Legends and Myths

◯ In the Middle Ages, stories abounded in many European countries about werewolves—creatures that were part wolf and part man—who would attack and devour humans. The Danes, for example, believed that if a man's eyebrows met, he would become a werewolf. French and German tradition held that a child born with teeth or in some strange manner, such as feet first, would grow up to be one. People believed to be werewolves were sometimes killed.

◯ The ancient Egyptians worshiped cats, and a person could be executed for killing one. In 525 B.C. when the Persian King Cambyses II attacked the Egyptian city of Memphis, he flung cats over the walls of the city. The people inside were so horrified and frightened by this bold act that they surrendered immediately.

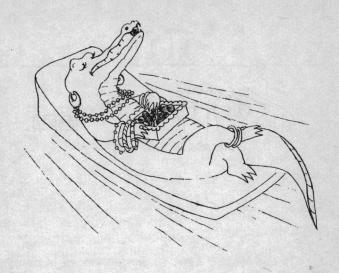

○ Crocodiles, too, were worshiped by the ancient Egyptians, and kept in temple pools, adorned with gold earrings and jeweled bracelets. Sometimes, if a slave was uncooperative, he was tossed into the pool.

○ Violinists once handled toads before a concert in the belief that the secretions of the animal would keep their hands from perspiring.

MAMA MIA!

◯ When the only surviving ship from Magellan's fleet returned from its historic voyage around the world in 1522, there were some unusual birdskins aboard that created quite a stir. The birds had gorgeous feathers but appeared to have had no bones —or feet. Stories spread about the amazing "bird of God," so special that it stayed aloft forever, with no need for feet on which to rest. The legend remained intact for more than 200 years, even appearing in a work on natural history by Linnaeus in 1735, where it was given the scientific name of *apoda*, which means "footless." Only after many years was it discovered that skillful natives of the East Indies had skinned, drawn, smoked, and prepared actual birds, never before seen by Europeans, to look footless and boneless. These birds today are still known by the name given them at that time—birds of paradise.

○ Manatees, or sea cows, were responsible for tales of mermaid sightings. These large marine mammals, seen at a distance bobbing upright in the water while holding their babies between their flippers, must have looked quite human to sailors who had been at sea for a very long time. Legends grew about mermaids, mysterious sea creatures, half-human, half-fish. Christopher Columbus, probably sighting manatees, reported in his journal that he saw three mermaids, but they were not as beautiful as they had been painted.

○ For centuries, powdered rhinoceros horn has been used in some cultures in the belief that it has magical properties. As a result, certain species of rhinoceros are nearly extinct.

○ The lively dance, the tarantella, was created as an antidote for the bite of a spider. In medieval Italy, people believed that if a person were bitten by a tarantula, or wolf spider, the frantic dancing would rid the victim's body of the spider's poison. Actually that European spider, a very distant cousin of the American tarantula, is harmless.

◯ One of the two teeth of the male narwhal whale protrudes from its jaw in an 8-foot spiral. In the Middle Ages, travelers brought many of these teeth home, claiming that they were unicorn horns with magical powers. Many wealthy and powerful people, always wary of assassins, used the tooth to decorate the rims of their drinking cups, in the belief that the "unicorn" magic would counteract any poison that had been dropped into their drinks.

◯ The stork is considered good luck to many Europeans, and some people even build nests in their chimneys to attract the birds as they return from their long migration journey.

INDEX

About the Author

BARBARA SEULING is the author-illustrator of many freaky fact books. She says, "This book evolved from the series of freaky fact books, but my interest in animals precedes the series."

Ms. Seuling spends part of her time in Vermont and lives most of the year in New York City with her dog Kaspar—"who is TV material, but we don't want to spoil him with a show biz career."